WARRIOR SOLILOQUIES

WARRIOR SOLILOQUIES

TRUDY STERN

TWO FINE CROWS BOOKS

Two Fine Crows Books
Ithaca, New York
twofinecrowsbooks.com

Designed by Don Mitchell
Cover and interior sumi-e by Michael Morgulis
Author photo by David Moog

ISBN 9798990054318
Library of Congress Control Number 2024936822

Also by Trudy Stern

Taurus in Lake Erie
Tea Leaves (portfolio)
Ghost Dreams

Warrior Soliloquies can be thought of as a collection of "First thought, best thought" writings, each capturing a moment of fresh, unfiltered perception of the world as it is: a "now."

CONTENTS

I

II

III

I

RAMPS

Now is the time when
deep in the woods
leaves of leeks unfold.

Ramps push back black winter's loam
green flags of springtime tremble
join my sack and head toward home.

Release their onion scent
perfume of the season
fills my kitchen.
In the soup to join potatoes, milk and salt.

Spring dinner.

Rose

We buried her placenta
near a fence on Trinity
by the old cherry tree.

This time we decided
not to cook it.

Next spring
a pink rose bloomed.

MORE ABOUT MARCH

A difficult month
I know that spring is wound
tightly beneath the sky
and frozen ground.

Long winters always end.
Today silent snow
blankets brown ground
and creaking pond.

Soon, April cherry blossoms.
Today snow covers
early buds
pink blooms wait.

MANISCHEWITZ PASSOVER

Who is advising this company?
Oh my God! (my "G" dash "D")
Really!

At the Co-Op today
a pyramid of Matzo—
yes! a sure sign of spring.

But not one box
of regular old fashioned
white bumpy matzo.

I know — I can get matzo
imported from Israel—
Shmura and not-schmura;
all certified kosher—
but Manischewitz! The source
for American Jews
of sweet concord grape wine
and matzo for generations.

In my Co-Op there is only the following:
"Mediterranean" matzo with salt, olive oil and rosemary
"Egg" matzo — I know it's been around,
but I've refused this newfangled stuff since 1955
"Whole wheat"— not exactly whole
but greyish brown and even more cardboardy
than the matzo that preceded it.
then there are Matzo Crackers
with their "unique, unsalted, six sides shape"
since 1940.

But what I am searching for there is none.

White Matzo with ridges and holes,
perfect to hold soft sweet butter.

This, Mr Manischewitz,
is why I became a Buddhist.

"Shmura" is Hebrew for "guarded." Watched from harvest to bakery. The extra level of scrutiny—and the labor-intensive process required to make handcrafted shmura matzah—is largely what accounts for its high price: anywhere from $20 to $60 for a single pound.

Summer Solstice

Days will start to get short
while the nights get long.
Fall approaches.
Lettuce soon will shoot to seed
kale bursting yellow flowers.

The month of Caesar now begins:
hot summer, long days, late evenings
sultry, simmering, sexy.

Last night in the yard
sweat rolled down my sides
just sitting, mind you—
no breeze, no air, steamy.

Sunset will be late with long shadows.
By 5 am it will be too bright to stay in bed.
By 6 I'm in the garden weeds.

Daily House Keeping

In mornings we come
out of the cottage
to see the work of spiders over night.

Webs sparkle in the slanting light
each a masterpiece of silken threads.
Some stretch from roof peak to trees
glistening in the lakefront breeze.

Webs hang from shutters to shingles
branches to chairs —
shining, waiting for their prey.
Perfect, sticky, pretty traps
where sand flies and mosquitoes
meet their end.

An old bent broom leans near the door
expressly for the purpose
of daily sweeping webs away.

ORCHARD

This used to be an orchard
next to our old house.
I thought it a castle.

Palace of time
beauty taken for granted
music in the wind.

A feathered home
of silent memory
remains.

The World was Perfect

The world was perfect when
I was the gifted child
who roamed vacant lots
and played piano
ran fast
did splits
and acrobatic feats of art and fancy.

Art pulled open all the windows
let in the air, the breath—
deep breath—
when latent asthma
grasped my little wrists
and pulled me in—
death always on my shoulders.

II

DAY ON AARON'S PATIO

Brick and ivy
summer city patio.

One table with librarians
us at another, writing.

Poems take shape
brick by brick.

Poetry opens the lock
of my throat.

Patois of poetry,
borders of echos,
excess fugitive clouds
of language.

Clouds of words,
clouds of dimes,
diamonds in the sky.

Cerulean dome over
the heart of Buffalo.

Heart of my heart,
waffles in the air,
sugar dreams,
cicada songs
in Aaron's sweet space.

Hot October day,
blinding sun,
where he schlept
and swept
before the poets came
to sit in warmth
and write.

She gave me a fine-tip pen:
join the poem to paper—
little letters, fine lines
and tiny insects
walk across the page.

She keeps handing me new pens.
points that vary with my words.
this one so far my favorite tool.
I'll write and be October's fool.

MIDNIGHT ON AARON'S PATIO

Midnight, quiet. Comfrey grows
and poke and ferns and mums.
Rats come out at night
To eat the nuts that drop
From that big old chestnut tree.
They leave tooth marks on the husks.

Rats party, party—
downtown dancing rats,
hipster rats
dance on Aaron's patio.

Every night in fall
rats dance and eat and celebrate
in the dark sleeping city.
Downtown dancing rats.
The hippest rats all go
to dance on Aaron's patio.

INVITATION

Come to dinner,
poet friends!
I'll make food
inspired by Alice —
celebrate the language
of our tongues.

My color is chocolate.
I do not love chocolate
like some folks do
but I will include
chocolate
on the menu.
Maybe mole
maybe cake.

Cooking is my poem,
parties are my song.

Bring folks here
and feed them —
hot soup will follow
nibbles,
maybe cocktails.

If you serve a great soup
nothing else matters.
Wine of course —
Côtes du Rhone
these November days.

My collection of menus,
lists of guests, starts now.

Damn gluten free,
damn vegan,
damn lacto-ovo-pescatarian.
I'll serve what I want.
Food for thought.

SQUIRREL SAVORS

Squirrel savors in the dark.
Thunder in the wind.
Seeds in teeth across the roof,
back to nest to sleep and eat
under frozen sticks
and icy sheets of new white sleet.

Underworlds are dark and warm,
hidden spaces under snow—
secrets in long winter nights
creatures curled below.

HABITAT

In dusk's deep blue sundown
two huge rats
amble to our yard
to feast on bird seeds in the snow.

Later, sunrise bunnies run
under and around the garden fence
followed by finches, sparrows,
a cardinal pair, and if I'm lucky,
the hairy woodpecker.

When the dogs bound out
the door to explore and play and pee
the wild things scatter
peering from dense brush.

Squirrels watch, twitching tails
from garage roofs and fence tops.

Somewhere close, mice huddle
under crispy stalks of last year's
crops, building nests
for springtime pups.

What Can I Make?

What can I make today?
I wake. My first thought is food.
I hear Michael grinding coffee
in the kitchen,
then lifting the lid on the puppy's
treat jar. when she returns
from her morning tour
of the yard.
We are so close, the three of us.

My favorite time,
this sunrise stumble.
We spent the night
and now arrive in a new day
where I will make food
and write and drink.

last night we threw an extra quilt
over our bed to keep us hot.
New day, fresh and freezing.

Sometimes I step into the yard
to check the latched gate.
Cold air wakes me
wind slips up my naked legs—

no coat, no cape, no boots
just me in my nightgown,
cold air, and puppy.
Early new day.

SNOW

First snow.
Season of cold.
Winter of pandemic.

Wet, it sticks
to branches and rocks,
to tall wooden fence,
to wires and doors.

Change
is the nature of snow.

ENLIGHTENMENT

I was twenty-one,
brilliant and young,
sitting meditation
in the quiet attic window
of the leaning old farm house.

An august breeze against my face,
I sat down and took my place
close to the sunlit window.

That house burned down November 10th,
burned to its basement core—
with forty cords of wood we'd stored
against the north country winter.

"It's a big one!"Andrew said
as he ran down the creaking stairs
ahead of rolling smoke and flames.
The second floor was gone
before we knew there was a fire.

We kept warm that winter
by cutting forty more cords.
At night we huddled around the iron stove
inside a plastic dome.

The wind whipped through that plastic.
By spring it flapped in ragged strips
like noisy prayer flags.
We were young and tough and hot.

But on that pleasant August day
insects buzzing in the fields,
I placed my foot upon a path
and touched immense benevolence

so intense that even now I can recall
the sweet grass smell,
the air, the dancing light,
the hum of bees—the joy
dissolving into infinite bliss.

I heard a voice—
no, I understood from deep inside,
under and over and beneath
my guru's laughing words :
"Trudy, brush your teeth!"

POTATOES

1.

Deep, fertile, smooth, homely—
especially great
when hot with butter melting.

Plucked from rocky soil,
taste of the pure earth—
clean as wet soil sliced with a spade.

Honest, plain, nourishing.

Under snow, under sludge—
pommes de terre—
jewels of dirt—

Cherished starch
through grim seasons
fed simple Polish Jews,
Russians, Cechs, Ukraine folk.

Like ships
that brought us to these shores.

2.

Empty bottle.
On the neck, Cyrillic letters
spelling 'wodka.'
Was the vodka clear?
Like water, like ice?

Tonight, it's ice cold in Buffalo,
very like St. Petersburg in March.

Wrapped in fur out on the ice
sled pulled by the horses—
all stomp, spew and steam—
he shared the vodka
from his silver flask.

You know the one—
tarnished sterling
now a century old,
sitting on a dusty shelf
In cold Buffalo.

Booze made from potato
skins to warm
Irish, Scotts, Poles and Jews.

Potatoes the food
wrenched from poor and rocky soils
by wretched souls
bending to scrape and pull
tubers from the dirt.

Comforting us
with brown and nubby tits
that fed our families on the brink
until we made it here
to Buffalo, Brooklyn, Montreal—

where we still make latkes,
while a forgotten flask sits
on a dusty shelf
in a well fed Jewish artist's studio.

ANCESTORS

Toward spring
I will arrive—
frozen shoulders stiff
with dreams of brute ancestors
huddled in their shelters
hoarding food and fuel
to last out
the cold season's cruelty.

Little shoots and tubers lie
silent under ice,
their fingers reaching
toward the sun.

Warmth and hope
will free me too.

In midwinter,
sparkling crust of snow
in blue light

warm poet
and tea steam rising
from my kettle.
Night comes early now.

III

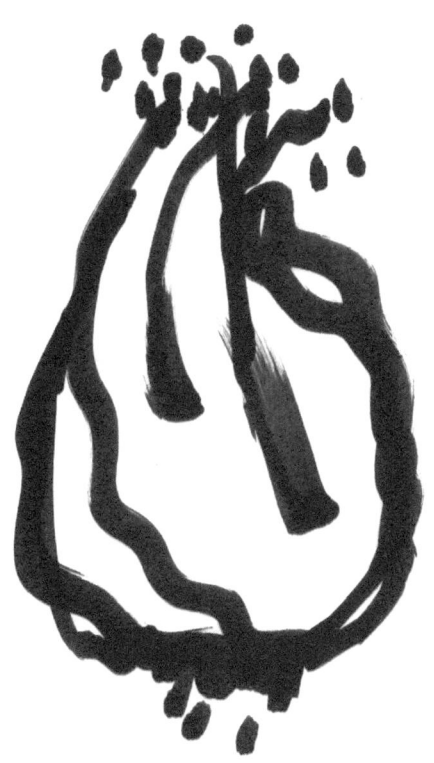

BLESSINGS

For Pen

I am very sad.
My friend is dying.

Black February snow
in shrinking heaps.

Bless frozen grit:
gray skies, dark clouds, and rain.

By the early light at sunrise
I know the year is warming.

Someday soon
there will be fur on the almonds

in the dazzling sun of Spain.
Blessings.

BLUE BIRDS

Flash of wings—
two mountain blue birds fly
from the frozen road,
alight on the branch
of a pine
to wait as I go by
in snowy powder.

CRACKS AND ROOTS

If you're not careful, you will trip—
stub toes on sidewalk cracks
where the roots of the fine old trees
are stronger than cement.

If you don't watch,
you could fall on your face
or your knees
or your outstretched hands

and break
a wrist
or a finger
or other vital part.

I spend my life fighting back
the roots that clog
our sinks and holes and tubs
and grow into tangles and traps.

They say that trees
communicate underground.
They touch and feel—tender
at first, then tough and thick

They'll trip me up, lay
me down, crack my skull.
One day I'll fall
and dissolve into dust.

STILL LIFE

Small lamp with bamboo shade
on the little table next to Junko's
ginger jar with the blue belly.

It casts warm light up the wall
toward the calligraphic scroll—
black letters with red chocks.

The gates of heaven open.

On the other side:
red sky, white snow, live oak.

An old blue plastic bag
skims up the street in the wind:
trash pick-up day.

ANGEL APPROACH

An angel approaches.
So this is death!
A shower of tears,
a lute, a flute, a violin.

Birds and angels—
things with wings—
hover in air, merge with music
seamlessly.

River of Words

Syllables. Weapons.
Breasts with names.
Letters, spears, bullets, milk.
My milk.

Like prophets
of the moment already here
in front of you.

Like tits. Rough nipples
expressed here
within my universe
carried on, through, over
rivers, rapids, falls.

KAMIS

Shinto deities called Kamis
are spirits that dwell in everything.

The little gods
of woods and animals and seas—
mischievous
or helpful if approached respectfully.

Wake up Kamis, wake up please!
I am sharply clapping, I make
an earnest vow, then deeply bow.

Some people call the Kamis
Muse. We sit down
to write or draw, and wait.
We move furniture, make noise,
procrastinate.
Hang mirrors, sing tunes—
Come Kamis, help me, help me please—

keep me afloat in the oceans of ideas—
too huge, too many, too rich, too much
too full of beauty
to whittle down to just one
little wavelet of inspiration.

Resilience

Rounding rocky islands
in a choppy sea,
you taught me
to sail into myself.

Damaged, ruined, wrecked,
my breath comes glittering
like a steeple reaching
toward heaven—

like a gladiolus
rocking in the wind.

HIGH WIRE

High wire, no net.

Life with you is tricks—
acrobatic feats unleashed.

I point my feet and dive
into your completely crazy pool.

TEA TEACHER

I watch her coming up
the empty street
heading to our meeting.
She walks an extra half a block
to cross legal with the light.

My friend Atsuko—
always well dressed
always neat and correct—
very Japanese.

Every time new.
Every time fresh.
"Ichi-go Ichi-e"
One time, One chance.

Wait for Me

Earth, wait for me!
Earth! Oh hot air, lava, steam and oil—
please stop.

How foolish to describe fools' gold,
carried out of view by the seasons—
dark, pure stones washed by rapids—

as getting dizzy, drowning.
Down to sparkling sands.
Carried, rushing, out with me.

GOD IS WATCHING AT THE GATE

God is watching at the gate.

Overcoats and feathers—
ears of roses hear the songs
reaching through loss.

Whose metaphor is this anyway?
Each shooting star is you
reaching through loss.

Light of moon on broken wings
limping down the street
toward Mutt and Jeff

who dance
on the edge of happiness
reaching through loss.

I am shot, a bystander—
spill blood and feathers
on gates of overcoats

and the ears of roses
while God watches
through the loss.

WINTER

Squirrels nibble
on stale bread and seeds,
quiver under the feeder.
Paw prints, claw prints
deck the snow.

Black capped chickadees
and sparrows
scratch and eat eat eat
through all the winter.
Thunder, wind, snowmelt,
snow dust and blizzards.

Prints on roofs
show squirrel was here.
Through the freezing wind
seeds in teeth
and back to nest.

A place to sleep
and squirrel away
under piles of icy wood,
black leaves—
covered by a new white sheet.
Safe and warm below.

Winter nights are cold and long.
Secret spaces, deep winter.

IV

SWIMMING IN ISRAEL

I swam in a country at war,
submerged.
Every water had a taste, a scent.
A different feel on skin.
Mediterranean,
Galileen,
overlooking fish farms in Carmel,
funky green pools near vineyards,
stinking sulphur baths at Ein Elat,
black mud at the Dead Sea.

Dissolve in dense water,
Then wash the salts off my body
in cold overhead taps on the beach

At the blue pool of hotel in Jerusalem,
mothers with head scarves in long dresses
wade and watch
their laughing children splash
while their husbands in dark suits
in nearby shade
sit on plastic chairs...
Young women in bikinis
nurse their tans.
American boys and girls dive in.

POST CARDS

1.

Dear poet
I'm thinking of you
this hot day in July.
I'll pack to fly
to Tel Aviv.
Dreams of sunsets
on the sea,
the beach, salt air,
burning boys and girls.

From my rainy perch
I know full well

outside, last night's rain
is sparkling in the trees
dripping from cool leaves.

2.

From Israel
Water the garden,
feed fish in the pond.
Bach on FM radio
is suddenly silent.
A woman's voice speaks
in Hebrew
somewhere there are sirens
saying take shelter
but not in this garden
In Haifa.

3.

Jerusalem:
Sandstone, sun, antiquities—
bustling cobbled streets.
Hasidic Jews with lots of children.
At bus stops in the dust,
narrow alleys,
sellers in their stalls,
Judaica and rugs
jewelry and food.
We take a break
for lemonade.

4.

Jerusalem again
People. Everywhere
echo of European lost.
Stones underfoot,
walls close around.
Olives, pomegranates
stain the cobbles.
Music, music,
songs of life—
shining chords
shimmering, resound.

ORTHODOX

Orthodox, what is that?

According to one set of rules.
Straight, upright.
Conforming to what is considered right
or true.
Strictly keeping a doctrine.

The very concept frightening.

Right not wrong,
not wider than the sky—
narrow like the marrow
in the bone, a strip of veins
running through a skeleton.

Narrow marrow—
suck it out—a special tool,
a marrow spoon
to pull the juicy treat.
Fat gel of meat
from the hollows of bones
deep inside the body
rich, gelatinous.

Marrow is kosher
If it's from a kosher beast.
an orthodox delicacy.

Flavor, they say,
accumulates in the bones
where none of us can see

the secrets
hidden away from eyes
in dark orthodoxy.

WHAT KIND OF PLACE

What kind of place
were the ships of God?
Little wooden boats
on perilous seas—

beyond all hope
somehow we survived,
beached on sands
landed below the cliffs
black seas behind
as far as we could see.

We were still alive
where trees took root
and grew into deep woods
to chop and mill
upon green hills
to build more
little wooden boats
and sail away.

After Birth

My mother's eyes look into mine.
I know that lake—it's fathoms deep
blue, dark, warm, fine.

"You sweet soul," she says
"You sweet, old, so old soul
I've known you since the birth of time."

Yes, mother, I've known you too
through life and life before.
We've had hard times and more.
Mother, I know your name is Love.

Here's our wish for this time,
this lifetime now—keep the peace,
the strength, the power of this moment;
cradle humanity in the Seed Perfection.

WARRIOR SOLILOQUY

These soldiers go for cabbage
as big as a head.

With bleeding ears,
sub-human—
their gods must crawl
on their bellies

like beetles
like insects
like gnats
like worms

crushed with disdain
like so many slugs
in the mud,
to blood and guts.

I live to crush another day
In the battle garden.

Advice to Myself

Don't believe
what you're thinking.
Look in the mirror.
Like what you see.
Believe you're as smart
as they think you are.
Rest when you're tired.
Be patient.
Eat what you like.
Brush your teeth.
Brush your hair.
Wash your hands.
Dance now and then.
Bow with dignity.

CZARDAS

Near a cafe on Allen Street,
violin music tore through the air.
A young man playing czardas,
crazed, ripping up his bow—
wild, like my father played,
the hairs of his bow flying.
The hair on my arms stood up.
Joy! grace notes! vibrato! sexy!
Then...no bow left.
He stopped.

CHARGING IN ORLANDO

Standing at a counter in the airport
to recharge my phone—
people jockeying for plugs.

Pillars with plugs,
chairs with plugs,
counters with plugs on each side—
people standing, sitting on the floor
with eyes on screens, and ear buds.

66% charged

Flight to Buffalo—ON TIME.
Orlando Airport Is:
little kids and young adults
with Mouse ears—
must be close to Disneyland.

Tonight I'll be home.

77% charged

Move to a leatherette seat
near a plug in a pillar.
Better than standing.

A girl with MU on her hat.
My first thought: "mu"—Zen koan.
Second thought, Miami University,
we are in Florida.
Third thought, Cow Talk.

If I feel better by dinner I'll eat beef.

78% charged

Boarding.

V

1969

Fell Street, San Francisco—
living in a closet on a mattress—
Motherfuckers' house.

Shoplifting to feed
the beautiful family.
Dancing to crazed congas
dangly earrings, swishy skirts,
dirty feet. Inspired
to smash monogamy.
Marilyn cleaned her gun
at the kitchen table.
Two babies in the house,
a little girl named Che
toddling, dancing, snot nosed—
one look at her honest wildness
and I tossed my Enovid-E—
it was the gun in the kitchen
that gave me pause.

I left for the Ozarks that year
to grow food
and live in a wiki-up
the size of that Fell Street closet.
To give birth to Sadie
milk the Jersey cow
live a clean life—
moonshine and army boots.

Ozark Hilltop Farm

At the Ozark hilltop farm,
a day like this—
blue sky and heat.
A truck filled with drunken
rednecks pulled up
on the logging road and stopped
in front of our leaning over
shingled house.

Moonshine brave,
white lightning stewed,
they came.
Yup, yup, yup—
macho drawls of redneck boys—
bombastic, boastful, laughing
so hard they fell off
their battered truck
and rolled on the red clay,
laughing to tears,
one rolled up and pointing
right at me he howled
"She's wearing army boots!"
and handed me the jug.

Fog Horn From the Lake

Fog horn from the lake—
mournful, open wail.
Some headed north to escape
with nothing but a butter knife.

What are these weeds
beneath our feet?
Green pushing through the cracks?
What survives in Buffalo.

Once were vacant lots
with weeds like these
and sparkling shards of glass
in pretty grass and chicory.

Cut your feet and knees
if you played not carefully.
Dangerous games—
cowboys and indians

with cap guns or just caps—
with rocks to pop and smoke
and smell gun powder.
I miss you, Buffalo.

Yawning holes with crumbled
bricks—all that's left of Ellicott
and Oak Street—apercu
of days long gone—glimmers

of the past. Buffalo, I miss you.
Ivy shadows dance on walls—
honey in my memory's vault
like a glass palace

with a fancy lid. I look back
at those times
when to my senses
all was bright and airy.

Magic Dream

He will saw
the Lady in half.
The Lady he'll saw is me —
long legs and lovely
in high heels.

I step
with grace
into the box.
Head and feet hang
outside the coffin.
Feet wiggle, head moves.
Pretty me — a bride.

I laugh and curl my toes
in those high heeled shoes
while he saws the box in two,
slips in the guillotines —
end of the trick

I step out whole
no longer a bride —
a hag.
A white haired crone.

MAGIC CURE

Dreaming is the magic cure
for all the ailments we endure
for war, for grief, for poverty
for my mind and body

For those who stood
outside the doors
homely, tragic, fat and poor.

Black curtains cover over sins.
College rules or wide blue lines
my solace. Imagination gifts
from desperation, days
of pom poms, plums and poet ways.

Your Couplets or Your Life

The outlaw poet
was insane, out of control
burning with outrage
her rhymes
throwing pens and pencils
at the moon—
sleeping, frozen, at the feet
of Emily
dancing on poets' graves
riding rough shod
through violent stanzas
blazing damned be beauty.
In the night
strong-willed verbs
become the angels' lines
dropping poems
from sea to sea.

Yes, There Are Also Flowers in Hell

Yes, there are also flowers in Hell
like doddering heads of sumac in the fall
when staghorns turn blood red.

In spring when pussy willows pop,
In winter when the wind is full
against bark beetle-riddled stumps
and ice coats branches.

Like fingers
like words
like life under ice.

At the cemetery at dawn
where time shifts through the
sound of water.

POETRY

I write poetry because
I can't trust god,

I trust words—
spoken, broken, token
all too soon
wheels of words roll on,

Folk trust poetry.
Loose noose, hang on,
loosey goosey,
rolly polly—
fools for rhyme.

Fools for time,
roll on, hold on, hold on,
don't let go.

Poems are life lines
strung from tree limbs.
Pump me, push me,
swing me high.

Hang on, little tomato.
Going nowhere.
Then I'll fly.

DESPERATELY NEEDING ANTIDOTES

Diagnosis: "Fear"—

fear of flying
fear of falling
fear of death
fear of disease
fear of bridges
fear of water
fear of spiders
fear of teeth
fear of poetry,
fear of books
fear of literature
(also known as linguaphobia).
fear of alphabets
Chinese
Urdu
Hebrew
A, Ah, Alphe Allef Allah Alif bet
fears that came
before the fear of others—
babel.
In the beginning was the word.

STARTLED DOVES WRITING PRACTICE

Thursday night group.
Paul's name in Tibetan
is Mountain Revolution Ri Sar-je.
Joe and Celia.
Come, friends, we'll zoom.
Let evening come,
my favorite time,
season of friends and language.

My favorite sad? Crawl into bed
after the cruel fight
and knowing
eventually he'll forgive me.
He takes a long time
meanwhile he'll tiptoe around
afraid to say the wrong thing again

My favorite happy?
Watching TV. Really!
Near to M and O
into a story with plot
with pretty people
with beautiful sadness
beautiful dilemmas or adventures
all resolved somehow
in two hours.

My favorite season?
early morning summer sunrise
long golden light
in the garden
cheerful zinnias bobbing
in cool breezes

before the rising sun
with Oatmeal my dog
who loves me unabashedly
while I drink morning coffee
and dream.

VI

Join my Demons

I'll join my demons for a drink—
a motley crew of writers
who meet on sixth street in the sleet
eat tsampa, cabbage, beans, and meat
get drunk on wine or Indian beers.

I love my fellow poets—
crowns of sonnets sit with horns
on foreheads
streaked with blood,

dancing princes in the storms.
Doors of perception creak,
blow off their hinges.

Hot breath before the snow—
still not spring, too cold, too old
if March is a poem it would be late
for now I'll sit here and wait.

PANDEMIC

She died the first of April
in the Corona year.
Masks were new
and hard to find.

She was too far gone
to know or care.
I sat upon the footprint
of her bed.

Her body slowly turned to dust
then blew away.
Last year of spending
dust to dust.

Hers was not a peaceful death
but cruel and hard.
Death crawled slowly
like a shade.

It was difficult.
She grew mean, not peaceful.
Not a peaceful death.
Broken down.

Death did not suffer fools.
No rules. Die, please die.
Gone on too long.Then
end.

GRIEF PERHAPS

I met my mother
in a chartreuse vault
the size of my small chamber.
Dimly furnished

with our past—
pink kitchen, blond oak
midcentury modern dresser,
antique writing desk.

A suitable memorial
for my love.
Was it love?
Troubled memories.

After Lockdown

We started hearing trains again—
wheels on iron.
Dreams of going far
rocking in this body.

I can hear them still—
they carry me into sleep
into day, into gardens
into work—
little winds
into my letters to you.

They carry stuff that built
the town, poisons from afar—
from mines in Bolivia and Tibet
build shiny finished trucks
and cars, blowing
 through the neighborhood.

Horns wailing sad all day
told me trains were running again
like blue veins
through the arms of the city

ANOTHER OATI POEM

For Celia

Our routine:
same each day—
crawl out of my warm bed
totter to the kitchen
fill the pot
light the fire
open doors for Oati
who dashes out to pee
(it's cold)—
30 seconds later
back for a treat
scratch on the door
patter to her day bed
while I get on my boots
my coat
myself
for work.

I call her for the WALK.
Out we go to watch the sun rise.
Dawn breaks,
every day a longer speck
of rosy light
scribbled in the sky,
red streaks the east,
while Oati poops on Wellington.

BEET BORSCHT

In my bowl this curious, complex
maroon, white, pink, red, almost black,
and cold...
soup.
Grated shreds of sweet beet meat.
For me, a small hot potato
and on top, cold sour cream.
Perfect and strange combination.

The rules to eat this borscht:
A largish spoon
To slice off bites of hot potato,
mix cold beets, their blood—
and just a smear of cream
to make each mouthful smooth
and weirdly pink—
potato warm, borscht cold, spoon-ful pink.

Every time I eat this summer treat
I think about the ancestor
who devised
this perfect mix of temperature
and taste and color.

Cooled her beet borscht in the well,
boiled potatoes on the fire,
waited for her cream to clot,
and came up with this recipe
which if you eat it right
comes down to one last delicious
creamy spoonful.

Blood of beets, fruit of earth—
sweet, sour
hot, cold—
crazy food.

DANCING WITH DAD

I don't remember the steps to the fox trot,
not that I ever knew them.
My father was a great dancer
and a strong leader. I just had to follow.

I don't know how I danced
in high heels and tipsy (thanks to open bars).
I just had to relax and follow Dad.

Stupid, horny teenage boys
never knew how to lead
but it didn't much matter because by then
rock and roll was happening
and dancing changed.

We practiced swinging, twirling,
jitterbug with girlfriends
or with door knobs.
I didn't like rock and roll much
but I did like twirling in a circle skirt
and sliding arms to swing into turns.

Rarely a boy could really dance
and lead
but mostly they were klutzes.
So I'd twirl away and dance alone
in the middle of the floor
surrounded by sweaty, smelly boys
and pretty girls.

A Loss is Unacceptable

For Ansie Baird

A loss is unacceptable in our world
yet we continue to lose.

The effort of the illusion that things
stay

is as useless
as the knowledge of which fork to use.

Poetry might want to get drunk
on the wars you carry in your pocket

skirting the world of adequate.
Loss may be unacceptable

but it's all we have to hold to.
Our wide Sargasso Sea.

"After Lockdown" first appeared in *Buffalo's Back: An Anthology for Our Times*, edited by Maria Scrivani.

Gratitude to:

Startled Doves — Thursday Poetry Workshop
and Saturday Poets at Fitz and Crane

About the Author

Trudy Stern was born in Buffalo. Author and artist, nurse and tea house owner and creative cook. Contributor to numerous anthologies, poetry journals. Never could be pinned down to one profession at a time. Chapbooks: *Taurus in Lake Erie*, Forty-Three North Chapbook Series, Saddle Road Press. *Ghost Dreams*, Local Color Editions. *Tea Leaves*, (Portfolio), Local Color Editions.

www.ingramcontent.com/pod-product-compliance
Lightning Source LLC
Chambersburg PA
CBHW030502130626
46549CB00007B/2823